Advance praise for *Something Wonderful*

Paul Jones salutes the world with *Something Wonderful*. This big book sings lyrical commentaries in sometimes lulls, courting parody; yet every poem retains a sensibility of good humor. Syllables bloop and loop and make light where a bird might plop or a snake might leave an empty nest. Every image shines, turning dross to sheen, as tinctures of evil sway unknown Truths among *Wonder*'s residue. Jones brings on the cicada's song, turns the radio off to hear tunes in his head, offers bright sounds in strains stars shine like skulls of ghosts. Humor? An ode to Krispy Kreme Donuts, plus a hymn to okra. *Something Wonderful* is just that!
—Shelby Stephenson, poet laureate, North Carolina, 2015-18. His current books are *More* and *Shelby's Lady: The Hog Poems*.

"Fire behind me and ashes ahead," Paul Jones says in "At Seventy," one of the many humorous and sharp-eyed poems in *Something Wonderful*. These poems, most written in the years when the shadows grow long, find joy in daily existence: "Gone are the little pains. In their place, just one ecstasy." This ecstasy does not result from "the three sins against your body—cigarettes, liquor and weed" but from close observation of a world that always offers something to intrigue us or make us laugh. "Could I remember you as my friend?" Jones asks the specter of death in one poem and that openheartedness makes this book noticeable in a season when many poets seem to be turning their back to those who populate the world unless those people commit to a certain social viewpoint and a set of behaviors. Jones would rather have his hammock meditation ruined by an animal than to simply stare at water, at sky. These are the poems of a man fully alive, a poet not only worth reading, but heeding.—Al Maginnes, author of *The Beasts That Vanish* and *Sleeping Through the Graveyard Shift*.

Something Wonderful embodies a vast, intimate terrain. These poems listen back through lenses of nature, variations of joy, sorrow, mischief, surrender, death, and a few constellations of mystery in between. Paul Jones perches the reader in limbs that were empty choir lofts. From this vantagepoint of his lyrical universe we experience the space between dreams, new worlds created by old words spoken, odes to tubers, donuts, and the magical everydayness of where poetry lives and is sustained. *Something Wonderful* offers poetics that are accessible, language that stirs memory, and imagery that overflows cups meant to constrain. This new collection by Paul Jones makes us swoon to a song about "a world where nothing that is cut bleeds."—Jaki Shelton Green, author of *Feeding the Light* and *All the Songs We Sing* with Lenard D. Moore.

Paul Jones reminds us formal control doesn't limit imagination—it frees it to spiral, to alight on Krispy Kreme Donuts, on porches, on red-vinegar sauce, on divorcees (one of the best persona poems I've read in years), on cat memes, and on a beached whale whose insides are 'a library / of what has gone wrong.' Jones knows how to beautifully staple down words. His language simultaneously holds and releases music, tenderness, curiosity, wit, and nostalgia. Something wonderful indeed.—Eduardo Corral, author of *Guillotine: Poems* and *Slow Lightning*.

Other books by Paul Jones

What the Welsh and Chinese Have in Common

Something Wonderful

Poems

Paul Jones

REDHAWK
PUBLICATIONS

Redhawk Publications
2550 US Hwy 70 SE
Hickory NC 28602

ISBN: 978-1-952485-46-6 Hardcover

Library of Congress Control Number: 2021948307

Cover illustration Kirby, W. F.; Schubert, Gotthilf Heinrich von; Society for Promoting Christian Knowledge (Great Britain). (1889). Via Wikicommons and Biodiversity Library.

Something wonderful for you,
Sally Greene

Table of Contents

After A Sudden Blow
—Responding to Jill Eberle's "Not This Time"

Swan feathers snow the hotel room.
What isn't to be seen is blood.
A plumed body, like a costume
Neglected after a wild night, floods

The floor. The bird lost his head.
Randy, Zeus-possessed, aflame.
Once animal. Then God. Then dead.
Yellow hair flashed at his doom.

Look at his beak; its colors bled,
Embossed, shaded like Celtic runes.
Did the manic bird-heart's dread,
As life left, blush her cheeks to bloom?

Just as she took on his power,
Our Leda put on his colors.
Vivid, not without pity, her
Eyes say, "I'll choose my lovers."

Against Bird Poems

The way poets go on about them,
you'd think birds were their inner lives.
Instead they're yogurt for breakfast,
no fruit, no nuts, no sugar, sour taste.
However healthy they are, they are dull.

They're one more trip to the ATM
to obsessively check your balance.
You get a couple of torn decrepit
Jackson faces for your empty wallet.
You slouch away unsatisfied.

You might as well stick your hands in
a drawer of unsorted knives at night
as write a poem about a contentious
wren or one more clownish titmouse or
that one indefatigable cardinal
fighting his own image in the window.

Last August, I saw a black snake curled
around an emptied nest in the quince bush.
Three firm lumps sagged in his body-long
belly. Flaccid and docile as I unwrapped
him from the thorny branches, he never
knew where he was being taken or why.

Against Desirelessness

The heart needs more than quiet,
more than a home without desire.
Sorry old masters, before I can let go,
won't I need to be holding on,
refusing to let something loose?

In my fist, I hold the aroma
of spring, of roses, of mown grass.
In my ear, I can still hear the creek
and the wren's song turned to scold,
as the snake comes down the tree
from her emptied nest. The touch
of the breeze as I open my palm.

All the Way Up

I used to dream of angels--
halos set at odd angles,
tattered wings and mistuned harps,—
sailing up from every corpse.

Might as well dream of dragons,
blonde damsels, and silver knights.
Even ghosts, ghouls, and suchlike.
The magic of death, much like

life, is too strange to make up.
At the last glint of sunlight,
when we are nearly gone,
I can see how things stack up.

It's turtles all the way down,
but vultures all the way up.

An Aran Sweater

I saw that sweater on Sunday night
in black and white on Sullivan's show.
Each Clancy Brother had one on
sent to them from Ireland by their mom.
How I wanted to be among them,
to be a wild colonial boy.
I thought a sweater would make it so,
make it so I could splendidly die,
romantically, away from home,
surrounded by men of the King's law.
Penny whistle and pistol in hand,
I'd take the first shot and the second,
my blood blooming through the mesh of wool
tracing the braided trail on my chest.
With cap gun drawn, I'd already died
both as cowboy and as Indian,
but for that sweater, I'd die again.
That's how little I understood then
of Ireland, famine, crisis, or Crown
or how the mother knew her son had drowned
in John Synge's play, Riders to the Sea.
The story that his wet clothes told her:
His sister, when knitting him a warm
pair of socks, put up three score stitches,
but dropped four of them.
In dreams, her son rode the fog-grey horse.
He, now ghost, wore an off-white sweater.

At Seventy

Days like this, I know I'm going to die;
I also know I'm not dead yet. I lie
in grass beneath the bewildering blue
where nothing seems new. I've nothing to do.
The idleness of age, as slow as clouds
on windless days, leaves less to waste. A crow
dives at dragonflies--not close enough for me
to focus on or to befriend. The dark
bird snatches light's glint. Bug-catching air shark!
That one bird keeps me company all day.
We share, even at our distance, two ways
of life: that blazing dart, my falling apart,
the opening, closing of our winged hearts.
Yuan Mei planted trees at seventy.
His was the slow way. So let it be with me.
I could get up and begin to plant trees.
Or I could just lie here on this green bed—
fire behind me and ashes ahead.

Beach at Corolla, NC

Inside the beached whale was a library
of what has gone wrong with the mismade world.
All the plastic jetsam in the Gulf Stream
swept up, sucked up along the wet highway,
sifted and sorted through the fine baleen.
Whose hunger ended when the tall waves hurled
that body onto unforgiving sand?
The one rotting, picked by crabs and gulls,
left at last like a bony cathedral
or the grit-covered ones who came too late,
the gawkers, the much concerned, the readers
of the tangled strands left as at an altar—
an opened book, unwelcome sacrifice
at the ruined edge of winter's paradise.

Bee Fall

Then the bees too tired to fly
began to land on our boat.
Singly at first, then in mass,
hail storm of golden bodies.
Wings attracting light like prisms,
like scattered mica. The lake
colored by refractions,
newly live, newly bee-lit.

Could we become part of it,
this storm of bees, this gold pond?
Our slow paddle through bee fall
took us places we've not gone:
past bridges, sun's failing light,
and song of life's last long dream
where friends meet for last goodbyes.

Can goodbyes last past parting
or are they, like bees' visits
to clover, intense moments
of working passion, nectar
searching, the sweet flight begun
soon after? Home to the hive.

But is the hive home? What calls
the bees isn't the wet comb,
sweet center of nourishment,
pollen piled as proof of work
done by all toiling as one,

but yearning toward oneness
pulled the bee storm to our boat
as summer's steam reformed clouds
made darker as each hour warmed.

Together for each other,
they left the hive for muggy
air. Their queen, somewhere among
the throb of flight, is ordered
by her wild disordered hoard

to lead their last pirouette,
their final sunset tribal
twist toward cold forgetting.

Above our boat, she was first
to look down, to make the fall.

First the beloved, then the all.

Better Tomorrow

From day's edge, I look back
Balancing the red of loss
Against the gain in black.

My mind construct twin towers;
And in pies I show the cost
Of how I spent my hours:

Twenty per cent on lust;
Desire for someone not here.
And the rest, on envy, lost

To rich dreams of repayment,
Careful castles in the air.
But dreams are installments

In buying down the debt.
Such dreams convert to words.
In words, actions have slept

Like armies waiting reveille.
I need only speak to urge
Them into a thunderous melee.

Then how to account for that?
Should I picture my revenge
As bodies dead from combat?

Or like Trajan's Column,
Troops from a looting binge
Twisting upward in solemn

Stone profile. Wealth and winning —
Even in the abstract—attract.
Folks say they aren't everything.

Yet nearer to the final bargain,
I find the currency of tact
Does little to requite my pain,

West of my window, a red sun sits;
That angry medallion
Glows before it calls it quits.

What follows but nighttime—
Darkening from vermilion
To profit at the bottom line.

Betty's Current Status

I've got a boombox I bought in 1985. I only play two tapes, Beastie
Boys and Nine to Five. I found it in the attic when I finally got
divorced. It's the one reason I'm still alive. That and a cat named
Beetlejuice and a son in California who FaceTimes with me twice
a week. And a check from the Bastard with whom I never speak.
Not even a check really but an e-transfer from his lawyer. Into my
account from that no account. I quit buying razors. I quit buying
Nair. "Grow where the hell you like," I say to my body hair. Not
that I don't care, but that instead I found some value there. Some
beauty really. My reflection wasn't their perfection anymore. I am
the one who can, after some adult pottery classes, turn mud into a
plate, into a vase, into a magic mask. The mask is a way to see and
be seen more clearly. The mask has one eye a bit cockeyed, nose a
little off center with one nostril flared. Not like the photo I had
made for Match. That one is posed, lit up, touched up, softened
up, made up, and smoothed out. That one got 200 messages in 36
hours. What took you so long, guys? The one message I might
have answered began, "I too have seen tragedy. At our age, who
hasn't?" I almost read it. I felt a kinship there, but a distant one like
the shadow image in a family photo of a forgotten third cousin.
I held the mask between me and the screen. "He knows how to
play the records, but honey you know those grooves too well. You
know those moves," said the mask. The mask ain't illin'. The mask
knows the truth. Some places it's all takin' and no givin'. Pass me
the scalpel and I'll make the incision. I make my own decisions. I
cut out the part of my brain that goes on suicide missions. I mean
Beetlejuice has his favorite box and I've got mine. I turned all the
mirrors in the house around so they won't shine.

Birds and Fishes

Because the world is willing
to forget what has crossed it,
the cold sea calls back salmon;
rocks glisten with their trying
to reach the potbellied moon;
we hear the tune of what will come,
the song humming near us yet.

The trees empty save one bird,
its head bare and raw as meat,
its dark wings held shoulder high.
Cold talk forged of cold words
would shield us, keep us behind
the brush jumble of our blind
while we watch the vulture eat.

Father, see the waters fold
as the stream unbraids, unwinds
having had its fill of loss.
Like a sail windblown to full,
this stream is set for the coast
where salmon leap and leave us.
We will never be their kind.

Birds and fishes came into the world
before Eden, before death;
so we pity these monsters
caught up in the current's swirl
Water or air. They dance stairs
over rapids, rushes and stirs;
action is their name for faith.

Our faith comes in reflection:
the clear mirrors of new ice
freezing all but the most swift;
the slowest held as if stunned
as if their rest were a gift;
the faster leap high as if
they could escape cold's malice.

What is here is without song
for them, from them. No vulture
celebrates the salmon feast
nor pauses to think it wrong;
what is offered and what pleases
draws the river to the sea.
What prayer could be that pure?

Our prayers start singing slow:
water seeping through the marsh,
the low rumble of the soil
settling in new furrows,
ice bridging the current's coil.
All that seemed impossible
sings as winter's wind turns harsh.

Blue Ridge

O Lost, Friend! O Lost, as if light and white
were one, the same river running through
the dark leaves. In green shade and green light
where our eyes move along wild curves
tracing swan necks down to the heart
as if they were remembering,
as if they were opening gates wide
enough for dreams to gallop through,
we are calm and still like snipers taking
note of the distance between our hopes
and our ambitions.

                  O grieving wind,
O banshee, O Time's wailing chorus!
We are not yet lost nor are we found,
nor are we saved. But for a moment,
ghost-like, we are suspended in sight,
held in crosshairs, prey to the patient,
hidden promise, that we shall return
someday unharmed and unadorned.

Bread

Pick up a round of bread and tear it.
All the mountains you see are snowy.
And the valleys too. The glow of it!
As if winter had been waiting there
in its regularity, its need
to own the earth, to remake landscapes,
a world where nothing that is cut bleeds.
The edges of this world rise like snakes.
Look closely and see their fangs and scales.
They're dragons at world's edge, always awake.
Some have grown brown wings and sweeping tails.
Bread's ragged edges are periphery;
the crust holds in bread's true mysteries:
the charmed life of yeast and all that entails.

Yeast's many charms, what does that entail?
Their gasps give bread its rising mystery,
gasses grown in gluten's periphery.
Neither plant nor animal, no heads nor tails.
Water, grain, and a little warmth awake
these beasts without skin, feathers, or scales.
In their house of dough, they writhe like snakes.
They die when bread is baked but never bleed
as their bodies build the unique landscapes,
mountains and caves, you hope for as you knead
wishing winter into the dough. There,
inside the browning crust, yeast grows in fits.
Yeast in half an hour make their snowy
scenes. Thank the yeast. Then raise bread and tear it.

Can Crows Kiss?

A wild wind
asked me this.
A whisper,
almost hissed
serpent-like,
each hard C,
the clack of
beak on beak,
misheard as
cheek to cheek.
But two caws
came later:
wove a braid
of rising
sharp music
that can pass
for the tune
two crows sing
together
on the wing.

Cardinal

The cardinal crashing into my window
can never love himself. His feathered anger
collides with his imaged others everywhere.
Each small injury, every loud thunk, the fault
of something or some red bird outside himself.
That scarlet stain and that fluff smeared on the pane
mark who is to blame for crossing the lines,
coming over the boundary of scrub pines,
count the cost of having to defend his nest.
And the rest? The birds in other windows?
Wherever he goes they are there full plumage,
full rancor, full stare. Insistent as thunder
crashing again and again, they demand
the clash of beak against beak, wings' fury,
sortie, sally, assault. He, the one who keeps
his own disdain locked in his chest, an unmapped
treasure both unknown and unfound, must attack.
He can not be done until they all fall.
They will not fall, until they fall as one.

The Church of the Misdirected Saints

I stopped at the entry of the Church of the Misdirected Saints to look at the carved doors. Images of small animals. Pets, I imagined. Comic as cat memes. Ferocious as their wild cousins. A paw batting at a bird. A fanged mouth carrying a lizard. A rabbit without a head in the jaws of a corgi. All of a savage cuteness. The kind that solicits an Oh! Then a rising note of Oooooh! Drop it! I said Drop it! Nothing is dropped. It's here stalled in motion in dark wood. Inside the doors, the sanctuary is unlit. Darker than the wood, than most nights. But one candle is lit. It asks me in. A fire from my own Misdirected Saint. Oh Dohn! (I forgive you for your respelling of your own name). You never killed anything. Never killed anyone but yourself -- slowly with the three sins against your body —cigarettes, liquor, and weed. The Stations of Your Misdirected Passion are along the walls: Your first visit with Tibetans in New Jersey. The time you tended sick pilgrims at Bodh Gaya. Until one had to tend to you. Your exile in South Carolina where you lived without electricity. Your first trip to Japan to teach American English to older dentists. The confrontation on the train there. When you were called, in Japanese, "a smelly barbarian." You answered in pitch perfect local language "It is your heart that will be my next meal." Staying in Japan. The waterfall temple that would also cleanse you. Your marriage. Bell's palsy. Your child. All about love. But complicated. The last tape you sent saying "I can't and won't write. Listen to this." It is that tape playing in The Church like a hymn. The coughs. The wheeze. Something about sumo wrestlers. The silence. And the return to hesitant speech. "I think I am finally On the Road. Call me Sal. I may have found Paradise."

Cicadas

I treasure what they have left behind,
These bards who leave past bodies dirt-covered,
Clinging, emptied, music-less, enshrined
On a string as I necklace them like clover.

I have collected an anthology of shells
As I hear them reciting the poetry
That they learned while in the underworld
Then of their climb up the walls, the oak tree.

In lonely moments, they speak only to me.
To others, they are untuned, warped violins.
I am soothed by their joyous cacophony,
Their chant as they suck life from leaf stems.

What have they left for us in their rebirth flight?
Poems from three worlds, hope beyond day and night.

Clear Channel

My grandmother staked
her lot with her signs:
Cleopatra Fortune --
Reader and Canary Breeder.

She tugged me to her side
and showed me her white bird.
Through her few teeth
she hissed her words.

The mildewed air
washed her swollen ankles;
she shuffled as if manacles
kept her there.

She dissolved into a chair.
"Give me your palm
and you'll dream
your true name," she said.

But I made a fist
and fled upstairs.
I dove under covers
with the radio's blast

pushed into my ear.
A signal
across the clear
channel carried

an earnest
Cuban voice
that warned of Reds.
Between ballads,

someone sold
olive oil, religion
and dark cigars.
A crackle came.

Then a samba.
Soon that stopped
and static grew
like the language

of the spirits
I knew Grandmother knew.
Half naked,
I half heard

a hovering
overhead
and nearly said
"black wings,

black day."
The next thing
was that song
beckoning.

I tossed my little radio
off the bed;
let canaries' songs
fly into my head.

The power went out.
What I knew
of darkness grew
as thick as doubt.

Against the blackness,
I held out my hand
until a step on the stairs
creaked "Grandmother."

From the cool air,
I took the name she said.
And the music of late
night bloomed glad.

Dividing Waters (1954)

Signs divided the waters
when all the creeks were rerouted
around the evangelist's
father's field and crops withered
as the shopping center sprouted
and red hills of clay mounted
in red dust and oily mists.

Even their hair was crimson:
men at break--the setting sun--
their hard work clinging to them
made them all seem one red race
but too soon they were replaced
--as if by some magic whim--
by clean careful concrete men.

What was to come next was grand:
a new J. C. Penney's store
with tiles that set departments
apart like pools of rain
that captured only one tint:
the boy's section was lime green,
the toys brown, sports blue and more.

My grandmother took me in
—I think I was about four—
and the grand old man himself
held the door as in we poured
to gawk at the full shelves,
wonderfully uniform bins,
and the tall tight-lipped women.

Thirsty in all this outpour,
I looked for water fountains
and found two flanking a door
one shiny metal marked "White"
and a white one called "Colored"
new but with a dripping drain
still the colored one seemed right.

I stepped up for a cool sip;
one hand bravely on the knob
thinking I had made the slip.
With a rough yank, I was robbed
of my try for those colors
and shoved over to the other
by my silent grandmother.

But there the water ran red.
My lips looked like they had bled
a blood common to all kids;
the drips draining on the tiles
ran into the Young New Styles
section like Biblical curses.
I drank deep and almost burst.

Early Fall New Moon

When I'm dreaming like this,
it's as if I woke up sober
and don't deserve to be.
Like I woke up to gentle rain
or a slow waterfall
after a long dry September.
Gone are the little pains.
In their place, just one ecstasy,
one immense pile of leaves
where children hide most of themselves.
They are hooting like trains
imagining I can't see them.
I act as if I don't.
I have already left that life.
But where is the new one?
The black cloud on the Black Mountain
will, in time, be the home
to trout. From rainbow to rainbow,
a path we all will know.

Eastbourne in May

We entered Eastbourne,
a night-life free zone,
where the benches were splintered
and the beaches were stone.

Residents with walkers
bent toward the sea,
like windswept boulders.
grey fog in grey hair,

a sprig here or there,
defiant, yet indefinite,
like England in May--
grey by night, grey by day.

Times past, this town passed
for a resort. Its time's
passed. Now May's taken south
in tropical climes

where tanned bodies glow
warm in the shadows
of fruit trees and window
curtains never close.

The Emancipation of the Mermaid Tattoo

The laser took her scale by scale
slowly moving from waist to tail.
She had never been meant for him.
He had led her out on a limb.
He kept her there under his skin
an arm's length away, still in touch,
but never close, never that much
a part of his core, his truest heart.
They both had had a painful start—
her arm on his arm configured
when newly coupled by pain shared
in their first joining. She, half gone,
left him pained again, half alone.
She became too abstract to be
more than a faded memory.
Now as she vanished in light's heat,
she found liberation, not defeat,
a world beyond the flesh, a fresh
incarnation, again half fish
at swim in the ethereal sea.
Relieved of his body's hurt and rage,
she dives to her sisters' refuge.
There among coral and tangled weeds,
they celebrate that she's been freed.
They sing from the brine's inky depths—
"No sweat. No tears. And no regrets."

Erasure

An old man walking in deep snow
Has just begun to disappear.
Is he someone I used to know?
An old man walking in deep snow,
I wonder how far he will go.
I hear he built a home near here.
An old man walking in deep snow
Has just begun to disappear.

Firing Pottery on the Night Before Winter Solstice

Birds are gone drab or gone south.
Oak trees bare empty angles.
Leaves brown the briar tangle.
All that stood green gone to straw.

Empty the dingy ashpit
into the zinc-clad bucket,
then watch for winking embers,
last light from the late fire.

On this night, we remember
each acrid taste of cold air,
last kisses that fall can claim.
Soon replaced by winter's flames.

Hilltop bonfires fight the night,
dark comes closer, stars ghostly
as skulls in unfocused light,
messages hung in stark trees.

Before the end of short days
when the sun again gains sway,
we turn clay, as seasons turn,
then we set our kiln to burn
new forms of funeral urns.

The Good Butcher

The good butcher ignores the bones.
He seeks out the soft tissues,
the parts that hold parts together.
He has set the saws aside.
He reaches for the broad cleaver.
It will do for cutting sinew,
for exploring the spaces
ligaments and tendons conceal.
Whatever holding on was had,
the butcher has disjointed,
disassembled, disunited.
Yet nothing is broken or hewn.
He stacks the once familiar flesh
in the cold room. Except the chest,
whose intact ribs, he hangs on hooks.

The Happiness of Fear

I am the gleaming skull with bony fingers,
the host pointing towards the birthday cake.
I tower over the party makers—
those hip high heroes—Batman, Elsa, Hulk,
Ariel, Mulan. They all cut and run
and hide behind the couch. Their mothers,
cats or queens or a friendly witch. Their fathers,
sheeted Greek gods unintentionally
cast as Bacchus with beer and dad bod.
Here parents are safe places to peer from,
hideouts to dash out of. Eventually,
the game becomes touching my shoe, to squirm
giddily, to contact this grim unknown,
the old touch-and-go tease that life lives on.

Homage to George Herbert

At that beginning, I
Was possessed by a ghost
Known too well as Want.
I was the host at first,
But soon the roles reversed.
I was, by my self, lost
Like a country parson
Banished by his parish.
And Hunger came so close
I became the owner
Of his name and he mine,
Unworthy any kind
Of friendship or of friends.
Then pain came to an end
At Love's wide open door
Ready there to receive
Me and lonely Hunger.
For us, a table was
Set to feed every need.
We, who strayed, sat and stayed.

An Honest Talk To The Shadow

Oh for fuck's sake. You're back again.
Bird, whose other name is darkness,
whose wings unfold like leather, black
hashmark, permanent bleak birthmark.

When the sun goes behind a cloud,
you light, noir avis, on near limbs.
What you bring are fear and omens,
harsh raven. Your chirps never sing.

Pitiless hooked flesh-breaking beak,
talons that tear too deep for scars,
shadow over the brightest stars,
could I remake you as my friend?

The wise say night, like light, can blind
yet both extremes can free the mind.

Hot Now!
— an ode to Krispy Kreme Donuts

They have no ends, no centers.
Angelically white, they rise.
They expand before our eyes—
light, lithe, gracefully bloated.
Hillbilly bagels begin their float
down the river of hot oil,
wafting, as we are watching.
They are casually comforting
as they fry—tan, taut yet tender.
Midway, midstream, they execute
their athletically perfect flip,
effortless as young gymnasts,
as surfers on white wave tips.
Half naked for now, unsuited,
half-pale, they seek an evenness
in tint. They take their sweet time
before they come to us hot
off the rollers through the shower
of molten sugar, a waterfall
of nearly supernatural
supersaturation. Their glaze
as we gaze, becomes opaque
like the windows on summer days.
I'll down a dozen before daybreak.
Even if I lost all my teeth,
I would still keep my sweet tooth.
If I die of cardiac arrest,
at least I will have had the best
last meal. Not that I'm asking
to die, but that's the honest truth.

How Firm a Foundation

"The foundation starts in the mud.
Just like Adam," Clarence explained
as we dug into hard red clay.
A part-time preacher who had killed
at least one girlfriend (True, she had
kicked down his door and both were drunk),
Clarence talked about starting over,
about solid footings, deep pits
set to hold the slosh of cement
that would harden to hold up houses.
"You get too far from earth," he said,
"and you end up too high to see
what's what. Like the painters next door.
Up on those wobbly ladders. They break
at three and go straight to A.A.
to get sobered up before they
can drive back home to Gaffney.
Then there's the roofing crew, all on
work release so you can be sure
they'll all show up. The chief picks them
up at the county prison farm
at seven. They start out okay.
Look at them now though. They've got some
Roman candles. They're shooting
over the roof line at each other.
House building is more like Babel
than most folks know. Last night, I dreamed
of the earthquake that is surely
coming, of the fires that follow,
of this neighborhood's shimmy shake,
of all these houses teetering
like idols before the ram's horn
blast back there in the Bible past.
All that was left was the pilings,
the footings. Sure, steady, like God's
promise to preserve the righteous."

I Do This. I Do That.

I stay in bed too long most days. I boil water when half awake.
Then forget to add the coffee. I'm out of tea. I feel the cold floor on
my bare feet. I could put on socks or turn up the heat. I do nothing
much. I worry about animals. Here and in Africa and the last cloud
leopard. I want to write a check to make their lives better. I'm out
of stamps. I want to call a friend who is still in Vietnam, but it's
noon here and midnight there. I call anyway. As if he could answer.

I Too Dislike Them

Aspiring poets are jerks
Who confuse quirks
With sound work.

Nietzsche was pissed with poets:
"They muddy their shallow streams
To make their songs seem deep."

But what of the strange ballet
Of words - rhymes like interplay
Of loves found and gone astray?

"They cause commotions," Plato
Said: "These poets have to go.
Their images are too obtuse."

Don't poets' images excite
Like small boats on the sea at night,
Flickering patterns of light?

In the end, nothing happens
As Auden's cold pen told us.
We survive, but won't transcend.

They were right, the Old Masters:
Poets are useless bastards.

The Impossibility of America

"I've finally come to grips
with the impossibility of America,"
Bill told me on our weekly Zoom call.
We check in and sip whiskey
and compare birds that come
to our feeders and suet blocks.
"The damn thing looks like
a pterodactyl and sounds
like a fucking jackhammer,"
I said about the pileated woodpecker
that woke me up that morning.
"He was a silhouette, black behind
the low sun, but his crest caught
the morning light and flashed red,
its true color. Just a little revealing,
and I knew then what he was.
I heard his cackle, like the cartoon,
like that Kay Kyser song.
My mother sang that song the year
she died. She was remembering
things that made her happy.
'He gives his rivals the bird,'
she hooted out and the fat nurse
attendant blushed red, but laughed."
"Getting back to America,"
Bill interrupted. "I can
only see it in darkness.
I can, like old Walt Whitman,
hear its various songs.
I know it, almost, but more
as a water-color of a memory.
I can't see the future in this light.
But something about it, something still
makes me happy, gives me hope."

In The Unripe Season

The doe had become too brave,
leaving shadow for sunlight.
Once when lusty, I believed
I would follow. In hindsight,
capture was no condition
for her, for me. Now I see
listlessness is all I own.
For me, shade tenders mercy.

The bold deer's remove to light
with no snort of refusal
is a kind comfort, no last
resort, no counter to flight,
but a restless recusal—
wild on the diamond frost.

In one hand, *mine*.

The other, *yours*.
On one palm, love.
The other, life.
But these tight fists
with fingers rolled
in defense like
armadillos,
have inside them
anger, inside
of that anger,
a new found grit.
Around that grit,
a pearl begins.
Open them quick
for a sharp clap.
Open them wide
to give a slap.
Hold them open
to form a cup
to catch the rain.
To catch cool rain.

In Praise of Small Disturbances

My mind is not quiet.
I may look like I'm resting
here in the hammock—
one leaf then another
joining me, enjoying
the breeze and fall sun.
But I'm not like my friend
whose meditation
was ruined when a frog
plopped in his pond.
I love a circled surface,
a fish leap, an insect skim,
each new connection to this world,
more than mirrored clouds,
more than the reflected sky.

Invitation to a Damselfly in March

Devil's needle your bright glint draws my stare
When your dart stitches the warming air
Two dimensional bog dancer
First fresh sign that spring is here
Head first you disappear
Neon streaked prayer
Light wind panther
Hunger spear
Land near
Here

Ireland Seen From a Porch Swing in Hickory, NC
—for Adrian Rice

Ireland is a country without porches.
What they call a porch is just an entry.
No one sits there watching for neighbors
walking by with their electric torches.
Their voices, soft as as blossoms, gently
fill humid summer nights with rumors.

Over there, secrets are shared in the pubs.
From unsteady high stools, the stories, tinged
with irony, rise easily as smoke.
New worlds are created by old words spoken.
Even the weightiest tales take on wings,
if only whispered above the hubbub.

But here, the slow news is told by moonlight
in the lazy tease of an August night.
Too often tea, iced and sweet, is the drink
that greets the blink of stars through the dark haze
as our voices wander, each twang distinct,
in the dog-starred nights and the torpid days.

It's ghosts that bind us across our weathers,
that tie the lilt and slur of daily sagas
told inside and out, in bars and open air,
to some episodic common drama.
They appear here and there, vivid and stark,
in talk that reweaves their spells in the dark.

Larger Concerns

Am I somehow less manly
for not wanting to shoot
rats down at the dump or
drink until I can't walk or
or vape or snort or inject or
jump on Jerry's ass over
a girl both of us would
learn was nowhere worth
a cracked tooth? Last contact,
she was a waitress at an IHOP
outside of Richmond. Jerry
became a professor who would
rather go to RenFairs than to class.
One of those who changed but
could not change his career.
Someone who researched swords
as if dragons were a possibility.
Jerry called me late at night
forty years later to tell me all of that.
She had come to see him at his office.
He answered the door in his mail shirt.
There was a stump with an axe
where his desk should have been.
Whatever she had come to say,
she took that with her as she left.
"And you, what's up?" he asked.
"Jerry, did you know that the
Universe is going to collapse
as it expands until gravity is
no longer consequential? Or
the black holes, whose attraction
is infinite, will draw everything
into a wad in which mass
vanishes and everything is
just dark energy? I mean, friend,
I have larger concerns these days."

Lewis Morley's Photograph of Christine Keeler Sitting the Wrong Way Round on a Copy of a Arne Jacobsen Chair (UK) 1963

The back turned to us (the chair's), the uncertain slant of light,
reveal and conceal, to a thirteen year old boy's delight,
hints at what had happened in the infamous honey trap.
Elbows hide her boobs, no shins shown, shadowed darkened kneecaps,
through a rough cut off-center handhold, almost worth the view,
a bit of bare belly. But even that is shadowed too.
Quaint now. That was a different time, a different world.
The chair, the winner, became more an icon than the girl.

Lost Harbor

What's held here?
Fog mostly.
Working boats
roughly shored,
hulls upturned,
season done.
Pleasure boats
tied too tight
chafe moorings.
Their sharp songs
louder than
early gulls.
Above this,
in hospice,
the death watch
for our dad.
We wait all
night to hear
his rattle,
his last breath
unharbored,
the last mist
to contest
the rising
brutal sun.

Lunar Explorer

"Now I am drinking the moon,"
Jimmy age six said one night when
we sat outside after dark,
when the crickets were crisp
musicians coming closer,
and the fireflies as thick
as stars were forming their own
kinetic constellations
as if eons were passing
just above the uncut grass.
Jimmy was tilting his glass
of Coke at an angle that
caught the moon glow, another
ricochet for sunlight
held for a moment in his
small tight hand. He chugged it
down then he made a sound
like a distant train, high
then low, then high again,
as the fizz went up his nose.
"That's how the rocket sounds
when it tries to land," he said.
He sat the drink on the table.
He clapped his hands loudly.
"Then it crashes in a crater,
but it's the moon that explodes."

Mellow Gorillas

Who gave the gorilla a doobie?
Who showed him how to inhale and hold
the warm smoke in his lungs? Hear the slow
sigh through his magnificent nostrils
as the cooled grey is released? His mate
sniffs him trying for a contact high.
Wide-eyed, wild-eyed, their love-filled eyes, rare
as four eclipsed suns at a spring noon.
They are laughing. They clasp each other
chest to familiar chest. Like comets
taking new orbits as they enter
a deeper space, they find each other
in new ways. New gravities pull them.
Is it all illusion? Some herbal
disorientation? Some celestial
prank? Just some dumb weed burning brightly?
In its burning, weed frees these lovers.
For a moment, theirs is the cosmos.
Friends, who try to live a purer life,
please don't judge this moment of escape.
Love, like meteors, falls in many shapes.

Messengers

They both came back unanswered:
my letter to an old friend,
the egret in the cattails.

Flat, brown-tinged, unstirred water--
silent as in past years. Then
the letter became a boat
for as long as it could float.

One, in time, flew further south;
the other has more to tell
under the willow shadow,
outside the cold current's flow

Moving from House to House

We live in a sacramental universe;
Every small act becomes an act to redeem us:
A brocaded coat repaired and handed down,
A kind of ancient music teasing the attic air,
The bats ganging up between screen and eave.
Sacraments hold us up when we fall down.
No longer dead rites, but buoyant, ebullient
As the dust of past lives settles after crossing
Thin bars of light. Light taunts the bats. It flies from
What's left of beads and silver woven into the coat.
But the music is something misremembered
Like postmen and doctors knocking at the front door,
Or the cool, but kind, last look from a head nurse,
Or the dark moon that calls "black wings, black wings."

The mundane but discreetly lovely details of our daily lives

The list on the refrigerator
gives all the signs of family:
peanut butter and tuna steaks,
garbage bags and red wine,
an offer to discount the mortgage.

On the sill, a reddening pepper.

The green side in shadow
with a crisp dried soap bubble
breaking the reflected light
like rose cathedral windows
warming the cold grey church—
hearts welcoming in a spirit—
exotic and solid as mango seed—
sweet pulp of these days;
like a map with too many details.

Gods of a world too mundane for gods,
you blinded me. Now you amaze.

So much, so small, and so irregular—
who will sing of you?
Who will tell your particularity,
your temporary insistence,
the way the pepper sinks in the sill
when overripe, how a drop forms
then falls from the faucet?
Only those who have been too wise
for too much of our lives,
who pause before you here
and for a moment know
that one beautiful fear.

For you, I will rise early
before dumpsters greet
their dump truck lovers
and are lifted in their iron arms
like passionate whales,
I will gather what is wasted,
what remains American,
and be forever true.

My Life as a Scorpion

began in darkness.
I was my own light.
The glow from within
was all I needed.
The faded blue-green.
The subtle pale blend.
By that I could see
and almost be seen.
My sting, a shining
poisonous lantern,
first coolness then burn,
was all I brought you—
the fire of knowing
what was soon to come:
your body swollen,
soft, sweet and tender,
before the hungry
tearing of my claws.

My Precious Death

I haven't been giving it enough
thought these days. Not like I did before.
Then every cough, every ache
flashed like a damn police car
demanding that I pull over,
that I present credentials to show
my organ donor status, my official
photo, my blood type, insurance—
the whole circus show of identity—
as if that was who I was, who I am,
who I will be when I'm laid out
and made ready to be laid down.

In the mirror, last night I saw the skull-
faced cop behind me. He had one hand
touching the brim of his dark and silver hat
and the other, yes I saw it, on his gun.

My Roommate Jeoffry

For I will consider my roommate Jeoffry
For despite being pretentious and a stoner, he pays his part of the bills on
time.
Except for the power bill which he considers an illegal tax.
For when he has the munchies, he will share his late night burrito with me
and any guest.
But as he is vegan, it will be stuffed with tofu and beans and onion thereby
making the offer one that is rarely accepted.
For he is a fan of classic rock. More than a fan. He played *In A Gadda
Da Vida* on vinyl on repeat for days. Until he misplaced the record or the
cleaning crew took it or he can't recall just now.
For he clips his toenails while sitting on our shared sofa which he will
clean up eventually. Eventually.
For while he clips, he cheers on perpetually losing sports teams -- the
almost-made-it-s amongst whom are the Cubs, Cleveland (even with
LeBron), Carolina football (both Panthers and Tar Heels), and even the
Hamilton Tiger-Cats.
For he will not channel surf from a sports channel once he is engaged. Nor
will he allow another to participate in such practice.
For he loses sports bets with dignity, but without actual payment of said
loses.
For he wears a vintage Jimi Hendrix tee shirt each year on September 18.
For said shirt has not been washed since 1970 on that terrible day.
For he reminds me and everyone he meets of this fact on that day.
For he spells his name not as Chaucer hath spelt his name. And thus he
pronounces it unlike any other person and expects you to do the same.
For his girl friends are cute and inconstant but not infrequent.
For he is often out of the apartment when they visit.
For they often want to share wine.
For once the wine is shared, one named Sally, whom I especially enjoy,
confesses that I am the true object of her interest and affection.
For Jeoffry does not trust me to feed his cat, Nico, although I am very reli-
able and Nico prefers my company to that of Jeoffry.
For he is traveling to Colombia despite State Department warnings not to
go there.

For he seeks "the only pot worth smoking."
For Jeoffry has only one key which he has left with Sally while he is traveling.
For he has asked her to check on his cat while he is away. And she has been reliable.
For we have gotten quite serious.
For he never holds a grudge.
For he is forgiving.
For he stays away for months.

On an Okra Flower

A pollinating wasp sliding
from white lip to purple darkness,
the shadow-heart so deep inside,
the plant, itself, tall African
in the kitchen garden's last row,
speaks of passage and endurance,
those far too common abstractions,
made real here in the summer heat.

Let it lead us, serve as a guide,
tell how each struggle leads to bliss
and what to bless when we decide
to see the past and present blend
into what we need to know
—a mind aware or in a trance?—
what to keep close, what to shun,
made real here in the summer heat.

What song can a wasp sing gliding
the flower's dark throat? A long kiss
like winged tongues tangled deep inside—
a blind passion, an obsession.
I hear it as a prayer now,
music for the world's whirling dance.
Sound, sight and scent. An orison
made real here in the summer heat.

Pairing Mantids

He has only one job to do. And she, with her hunger,
her need to feed the future without him by consuming him,
has a lot to get done before winter.
His head tilts slightly, like a sinner at communion,
like a teen expecting his first kiss to be like lightning.
Then his body starts to do the work it was built to do.
She turns toward him and wipes off his face.
He knows it's all over, but his body keeps on, unknowing itself.
His is the kind of stupid happiness
you can only appreciate at a distance,
the kind you know cannot be as good as it looks.
Hers is the work of duty and a different devotion.
While he takes her from behind, she takes him
head first just like she took a yellow striped hornet
who would have taken her to his own hideaway,
just as she took the grasshopper who was tired of summer,
as she took the large green moth who had no mouth of its own.
She ignored those magnificent wings—just let them fall—
as she ignores the thrusting body that falls away from hers.
He dies two deaths at once, the deaths of love and of life.
But the moment between, the moment before it all ends,
is the moment of his glory and the beginning of her toil.

Pig's Eyes

Most people have us take them out so they don't explode when you're cooking whole hog. In the pit, it's not too bad. A little loud sometimes. And the mess looks like tears on the pig's face. But cooking head-on on a spit is another matter. The first time I ever saw a pig's eye explode, the juice shot about ten feet and left a hot smear up the back of the host. He had been there since dawn drinking and turning the spit. Mostly drinking. He had no idea what had happened. He fell on the ground. He ripped his shirt off. He finally vomited. Of course, none of that helped. So we let him lay there for a while. His wife was over on the other side of the fire making out with his brother. She didn't seem to notice a damn thing that happened. When she finally did, she took a stick and poked out the eye that faced her. It oozed a little. And left those tears I was talking about.

Poem in Which I Forget Myself

What there was of pain has passed.
Recovery like a slow snow melt
proceeds while I sleep but rain,
unseasonably warm,
digs ruts then rivers. Outside,
in a world beyond my body,
a large world is being remade.
The moon must be in every drop
on every fallen leaf by now.
The moon must be broken light
in every new water flow.
Beaded and beautiful darkness
speckled with the promise of dawn,
too pure to resist like love's
impossible lure, like the space
between dreams, empty and wanting
footprints just as the night's river,
unaware of its banks, wants a boat.

Prayer to a Deer in Summer

A large buck nooning in azaleas,
his felted rack too early for points,
brown stalks erupting from the bushes.
Leafless, but in their way, they are lush
and wave as if wind disappointed
by the heat and by the rain's failures
to bring relief had appointed him
as the custodian of coolness,
keeper of hope in humidity,
the one who with one swift head-twist
could lift this midsummer fist of flame
and turn the sun from fiend to friend.
I call you from your sleep, take pity
on us, bring this swelter to an end.

Red Clay Way

Here vowels form the furrows,
bite deep into the red clay,
stretch their length across the field.
Words seem relaxed, more real
after working a full day;
they try to ask what we know,
what we plan for tomorrow.
The slow roll of what we say
is homed in the land we till.
So many of us, by now,
have wandered far from the plow.
In our other lives, some sounds stay,
still reach back to early speech,
to the stories we must tell
that follow us like hellhounds
that will never lose our trail.

The Red-Vinegar Sauce

So much depends
upon

the red vinegar
sauce

dribbled on pulled
pork

beside the white
coleslaw

Rising With the Moon on Advent Eve

This full moon on Advent's Eve,
God's eye for those who believe
that light seen over the eaves
is too pure a true bereave-
ment, that torn dark can't deceive,
but leads us from fallen leaves,
to fires and unperceived
flares in the cold air, reprieve
and punishment for naive
stumbles, missteps, those years we've
--till now--held close but must leave
to find their fate reconceived
as something sinless, achieved
in lunar reflection, grieved,
gathered like harvest, received
and tossed, heaven hung in sheaves.
For did not Christ hang with thieves,
hang like the moon--lights retrieved,
both at one and apart, cleaved
in both senses, unaggrieved?
When such goodness is received,
light refracts and love relieves.

Saint of the Trees

What is the proper sacrifice
To please our Lord, the Saint of Trees?
I asked the ferns for their advice:
What is the proper sacrifice?

"Lie here and dream of paradise,
Sink into the soil like the leaves.
That is the proper sacrifice
To please our Lord, the Saint of Trees."

Same Jay Seen Twice

I have not forgotten the way
a bright blue jay can change a day.
A month ago, he shook down snow.
He knew not to break into song,
but clicked his beak: "Nothing is wrong."

Now it's spring and he, being wise,
makes the greening limb fall and rise.
He jeers, he chortles, and he squawks.
I swear I hear him try to talk,
then mock his enemy, the hawk.

Scavengers

Nearly three hours to the coast, yet,
a congregation of seagulls
gathers in Bojangles parking lot.
Even in the retirement home lobby,
we hear their croaking, their squalking spats,
their little angers They won't let up.
They won't leave, even though the wind
has eased and the dumpsters were emptied
as light came on the oil stained cement.
The parking lot looked like a marsh
then, spackled light bringing birds back,
and the winter air holding down odors.
Almost a place of hope, new beginnings.
We know about bogs, wetlands, shallows:
what gathers there is seeping slowly
into some deeper water, blue
and like the sensation of late love
—eventually— enormous.

Seventy Three

When in time frost found me, leaves were gone yellow
or fallen or few on branches or fallow
fields. Limbs were empty choir lofts. Youth's bright birds sang
then left before the cold November must bring.
I found myself in twilight, the glow on snow
or rime on those brown stems or white wisps of breath
—how many more before death plants me below?—
But here I can see further, here my life's breadth
forms a vista. Here where flames once leapt, grey ash
is heaped, warm still from what past fires I've known.
Still all this going is not completely gone.
Something of those late bird songs will stay, will last.
What we see in age makes all we love more strong,
knowing what we love we leave before too long.

Skinnydip at the Millpond

Naked again and no moon.
The pond's surface fully starred
and we there between two skies.
The water sun-warmed, the air
too held August heat that night.
On the far shore, four horses.
Even in the dark, their necks,
their heads, seem light and floating
despite the drab drape of pines,
the dismal crowd of pin oaks.
As if fire were in them,
their heads shake as they see us.
Their wild manes, dim torches,
burn for an apocalypse—
a beginning and an end.
They seem to beg us to swim
through the wet constellations,
to mount them and take new names.

Slugs

They are so unlovely and unloved.
Yet they climb to the highest ledges.
Splendid rainbows mark their night travels.

One came across the axe blade I left out.
There was no dew on the silk slime
that ran the cutting edge this morning.

I would rather be cold and open
to beauty than let my need for work
and heat disturb that highway of joy.

Something Wonderful

"Let me mention something wonderful,"
she said, "Bats eat darkness."

"I see them shadowing the streetlight,"
I said, "diving to feed.
Like hungry fish in a small light pool,
they leap out of darkness
as if breaking the water's surface,
as if, for a moment,
that alien world, that other, was their home.
Bats feed as darkness breaks."

"No, bats break into darkness to feed.
Light warns them 'you can't stay!'
Think fireflies at the end of the day.
Their lights shine bats away."

"But aren't those lights a begging to breed?
Not just a sign of bitter taste?"

"As with passion, they say 'Come here'
and 'Keep apart' for now."

"Right now, bats break the darkness to feed.
Fireflies flash to breed."

"Each rules their own kingdom—darkness
makes a boundary to break.
Some dive, some flash to mark the edge.
To transgress is to bless
the penumbra, the lie of difference.
Don't we rise from earth?
Isn't our time soaring in this life
a flash, a hope for love?
We see the lures, but know we must
be feed by darkness and
are born with a taste for bitter light.
The sweet then bitter light."

Song of Joy

Joy is here!
It may be
insincere.

Chickadees
sing out what
seems to be

a song sweet,
not fear nor
tortured tweet

in defense
of their nest
in the dense

thorn thicket.
Is it love
when we get

songs from wrens:
"Joy is here!"
then they end?

They may be
insincere,
seems to me.

What the heck.
"We murder
to dissect,"

Wordsworth wrote
when writing
got his goat.

On some nights,
an untrue
love delights.

Insincere?
It may be.
Joy is here!

Start the Game
— for my Father

"Start the game. Start the game," he said
as he lay in the hospice bed
a starched pillow under his head.

Seventy years he had been wed;
he lay not far from his marriage bed.
"Start the game. Start the game," he said.

For four days, he had been unfed.
Only new sensations were nurses' treads
and a starched pillow under his head.

"Three. Two. One," his muttered count pled.
I clearly heard him through his meds.
"Start the game. Start the game," he said.

His eyes turned from blue to dry red.
He lay closed, like a book well read,
a starched pillow under his head.

Death's not what we hope for. Instead,
death was something he did not dread.
"Start the game. Start the game," he said,
a starched pillow under his head.

Still Waters

I am still, waiting
for the one moment
that old Eastern sages
say gives absurdity
an absolute clarity,
the moment multiple
bald monks chant to induce.
They say the Way is
like water. It will work
its wonders at due time,
the way water always
breaks up rocks, turns them
into sand, but will not
be transformed itself.
Being water, it's
already what it needs
to be. Winter and ice
merely redefine water.
Wind, when it works, only works
on the surface of water
When fire meets water,
water is sent to heaven
but fire just becomes ash.
Water like saints' returns
to perform its steady work.
Sleet, snow, rain or hail—
even fog—are water's
temporary bodies.
In time, water will be
all part of one huge sea.
Water will save us all
in time. In time, they say.
In the meantime, be water
as best you can be. Me?
I am still waiting
for all waters to become
still, to run deep, and
clear a few things up.

Swifts

They may as well be smoke itself rising
as they do from chimneys, ember-eyes
sparkling amber, their sooty silhouettes
like some precious dream unrealized.
Their hard high-pitched chirps not unlike fires sing;
their crackle carries songs I can't forget,
a sound that sits inside me, warming me
like early spring's sunlight, like their clouding
columns as the sun settles in the trees.
Even as their flight inks the red sky,
even as their swoops and dives disguise
their aims, these drab blunt birds in smooth flight
claim the air from bats, from owls, at moonrise,
the edge of day into unsettling night.

They edge the day as they unsettle night
with flaps and darts and swerves and surprise
twists. Something about them is not right;
one wing then the other oars the air.
Peterson called them "Flying cigars."
Flame-born, they are what's left of desire
after the heavy ashes fall to earth.
They soar to rewrite the cloudy white
at boundaries of blue. Dusk takes on their hue;
signatures sharpen then blur into blots
in the vast western sky there where red
sun's fire can be last seen and the moon,
refracted, opens to the world of dreams
that might well be smoke itself rising.

This Old Dog

This dog is too old to find the porch.
He's sleeping in the yard on the hard
stone pocked ground under the gum tree.
All those fallen prickly gum spheres
dig in his fur like a truck stop
masseuse just back from the nail parlor.
It feels so good to him, but he knows
that there is something wrong going on,
something askew in the system,
a broken connection maybe,
something saying this feels so damn fine,
but you know you'll soon be paying more
than you should. Just for now, let the sun
warm his tattered coat, his sore flank.
Let gum balls do their questionable
labor as he runs in his sleep
toward a rabbit he'll never catch.

Ode to a Certain Feeling of Optimism

Russell says I shouldn't trust it.
I should know by now.
Soon enough it will let me down:
one more dent in a lovely old car,
a scratch on my favorite glasses,
a friend who doesn't make the right choices,
too much hot sauce, which I love,
but should know the consequences.
"Excess is its own reward," I want
to tell him. "And excess of hope,
can that even exist?" I hope not.
I hope that I can find a way
to share this feeling, to say:
"That next cup of coffee won't be burnt;
it will never need cream or sugar.
That my parents are in a better place;
their late pains having paid their dues.
That they were allowed to enter
whatever afterlife can afford them."
Here's my certain feeling
of optimism. I want to share it
with all of you. I don't want
to shake it. It stirs in me
like a deep muscle flexing,
each time I can pass it on.

To A Tuber

The appeal of peeling you, Earth Apple,
is ample. For example, your worth,
your girth, once unearthed is a source
of mirth, of pealing laughter
of the coarse kind. Oh dirty mind!
Oh Unberthed Joy unwind! Hereafter
we name you: Mister. You poor tater.
Our inside joke. We poke at your eyes.
Then, pale Peruvian traveler,
we revel, as we unravel your suit.
Our peelers unclothe you in pursuit
of your whole reveal, Swollen Root.
Unrushed Irish, although you're slow to grow,
we don't regret we get to know you through
stew, roux, and ragout. Oh Spud! Oh Ground Fruit!
We love the cry as you fry, fatty thin chip;
you satisfy when paired with paté and dip.
Mashed, hashed, browned, knished, Tot-ed, scalloped,
whipped and delivered in white dollops,
flaked, twice baked, riced, diced, steamed,
microwaved, roasted, toasted, caramelized,
in mayonnaise, dauphinoise, or au gratin.
Your good taste races to paste our waists;
at your demand, we expand, unmissed
and unmanned, as wide as Gondwanaland.
When hot, you are passed hand to hand.
When small, you don't matter at all.
When we no longer crouch on our couches,
may we be found like you, Garden Gnome,
unsoiled and above ground, made right,
unspoiled by the night's shade, de-vined,
no longer hidden or forbidden.
You are risen, Rhizome. All is forgiven.

Ode to Very Small Devices

As fairies for the Irish or leeks for Welsh,
it's the secret lives of small hidden machines,
their junctures, and networks that inspire me:
Mystic hidden functionaries that make
our made world live, brave little servo motors,
whose couplers, whose eccentric fire-filled
sensors are encased in bakelite with brass
screws, who stare with red eyes, who gauge moisture,
who notice tiny motions and respond,
whose cooling fans call out in white-noise
registers like older folk singers—I can
almost hear their earlier songs, their strong voices
now yelps, their thumps, their throbs, their hum, their chant—,
they click, they whir, they are sent spinning
inside like teen girls giggling over boy bands.
Most of all: ones waiting silently, concealing
the surprise of their purpose, tasks not yet known,
their true natures found only in connections.

Those that listen, those that speak,
those that control cool and heat,
those that open doors, those that lock
all the things that we've forgot,
those that hide, those that disclose
those embedded in our clothes
those in our ears, those in our hearts,
those that bring together, those a part
of divisions, those like birds,
like parrots that complete our words,
those like fish, those that entrap,
those that free, those that freely flap
in fierce winds, those that replace
what we have lost, those that see
at night, in fog, in brightness, in fear,

those that show what we hold dear,
those that tempt, those that repel,
those that buy and those that sell,
those that keep us alive, those that
don't, won't, couldn't and cannot.

Parts of one mind, not mine, blunt orchestra
of information, bundles of feelers
reaching out to touch us, teach us, guide us
to form better futures better understood.
May your sounds, your chimes, your silence calm us.
May your tender tendrils touch what we seek.
Small parts becoming one being intertwined,
a world in itself, remind us to be kind.

Traces of a Portrait of Che Guevara on a Wall in Oaxaca

All that is left of Che are his radical eyes.
Weather and other graffiti took his beret,
but left its red star newly tattooed on the thigh
of a marching nearly nude, but clearly angry,
teacher on strike. Che's eyes are supportive, averted
in the kind of kindness our better elders
show towards the casual way their youngers treat
their brief moments of beauty and power and grace.
The marchers on the wall are so tall, so certain,
so committed. Che sees that he's fine without hair,
or nose, or lips. He is happy with what he sees:
their large homemade signs, their leaderless unity,
their hard won solidarity. Che had gone alone.
He had held the wall for so long, setting the pace
for revolutions. Now he has begun to vanish.
Still his stare sustains his power without his face.

Unnamed Early 20th Century Burial in St Matthew's Episcopal Church Cemetery, Hillsborough, NC

A small grave marked "Unnamed"
Without date or acclaim,
Past century's mystery,
Performs a ministry
Of grace in this churchyard.
This modest slab set hard
Against the worst weather,
Something meant forever,
Became grief's darkest gift.
A still birth swiftly shifts
Love from cradle to grave.
Was this small life unsaved,
Unbaptized and not named?
So pure life was reclaimed
Before life could begin,
Before the curse of sin.
Yet love with that life stayed.
Where roots have made a braid,
A resurrection fern
Each rain, in green, returns.

Verse in Which I Should Probably Be More Charitable Towards the Gift of a Book of Mediocre Verse

Every poem ends
with a reflection:
a fox or a deer
or a bird outside
the office window.
The lines before that
describe or hint at
some guilt or sad loss,
a breakup or death
or in a rear view,
a child teetering
on her tricycle,
taking a comic
fall, as her newly
divorced father drives
away. Before that
his memory of
a double rainbow,
now a phantom that
opens his heart like
a small fist that fits
just between his ribs.
The fist can not grab,
or clutch or hold on.
But it pounds as his
heart pounds, fluttering
like a golden bird
that an owl devours
at the dangerous
last hour of darkness,
first hour of daylight.

"So much bravery
here," an old friend said
when she popped by to
drop off tomatoes

and this dog-eared book.
One poem begins:
"I begin inside,
inside a grey stone."

When the Shadow Took the Day Off

Because the sun wasn't bright,
the shadow had no chores.
He slept in. That felt right.
He let the time go by.

Amused by his own snores,
like a loud lullaby
he had not heard before,
he got up up and brewed

a few cups of green tea.
The steam rose and entwined
like thick muscadine vines.
Maybe chocolate too?

"Well, Don't mind if I do"
What liberation! Not
to have to do as told.
What about a nice stroll,

a nice walk to the park?
Meaninglessness feels nice!
It was cloudy, not dark.
At the corner, he stopped.
Flashing signs invited
him to cross. "Walk with light."
He watched as they changed. Twice.

Who Would Not Celebrate the Changes

Who would not celebrate the changes
in water on a fall day. The mist
caught in drab shrubbery's thorns at dawn.
The rain ruling light as day goes on.

The range of it! Slipping into mud,
dripping from broad leaves, rivulets
in their moving hiss as they twist,
their calm pooling, their smoothed surfaces.

By late afternoon, it's almost gone,
taken completely by root and soil.
Save the glisten kept in crevasses
of grey gravel that will by dusk

be gathered up—grit and pebble
under a skin of ice, before frost
begins to beard and bespeckle
the moonlit husks of bent brown grass.

Acknowledgments

101 Words.
I Do This and That. March 9, 2021.

2River View. 25th Anniversary Issue.
In Praise of Small Disturbances. September 1, 2020.
In an Unripe Season September 1, 2020.

8 Poems.
Verse in Which I Should Probably Be More Charitable Towards the Gift of a Book of Mediocre Verse. 2021.

Adirondack Review.
Traces of a Portrait of Che Guevara on a Wall in Oaxaca. Summer 2021.

American Journal of Poetry.
I Too Dislike Them. January, 2021.

Anti Heroin Chic.
This Old Dog. April 2, 2021.

As It Ought To Be Magazine.
Something Wonderful. December 23, 2020.

Blake-Jones Review. now South Shore Review
Messengers. December 2019.

Broadkill Review.
Betty s Current Status. January 1, 2021.
Moving From House to House. March/April 2020
Seventy Three. March/April 2020.

Carrboro Free Press. Special Trash Edition.
The mundane but discreetly lovely details of our daily lives. 2009.

Cider Press Review.
Cardinal. Summer 2021.

Deuce Coupe Poetry.
The Good Butcher
Lunar Exploration December 9, 2020.

Ekphrastic Review.
After A Sudden Blow. March 11, 2021.
Lewis Morley's photograph of Christine Keeler sitting the wrong
way round on a copy of an Arne Jacobsen chair (UK) 1963. July 22,
2020.
Unnamed Early 20th Century Burial in St Matthews Episcopal
Church Cemetery, Hillsborough, NC (2020). September 8, 2020.

Grand Little Things.
Cicadas. July 21, 2020
Eastbourne in May. October 28, 2020.
Erasure. February 5, 2021.
Homage to George Herbert. May 20, 2021.
Invitation of a Damselfly in March. May 20, 2021.
Prayer to a Deer in Summer. July 21, 2020.
Same Jay Seen Twice. May 20, 2021.
The Saint of the Trees. February 5, 2021.

Hermit Feathers.
Blue Ridge. 2019.
Lost Harbor. 2019.

Light.
My Roommate Joeffry. 2018.

Indelible. Food and Nurture Issue.
Bread. May, 2021.
To a Tuber. May, 2021.

Literary Yard.
Against Bird Poems. February 27, 2021.
An Aran Sweater. February 27, 2021.
Emancipation of the Mermaid Tattoo. February 27, 2021.
Larger Concerns. February 27, 2021.

little death lit.
All the Way Up. Issue 5. Fall 2020.

Live Nude Poems.
Mellow Gorillas. May 24, 2021.

January Review.
My Life as a Scorpion. April, 2021.
My Precious Death. April, 2021.

Kakalak.
The Red Vinegar Sauce. December 2019.

Madness Muse Press.
Who Would Not Celebrate the Changes. October 11, 2020.
In one hand, mine. October 11, 2020.

News & Observer.
Song of Joy. December 31, 2006.
Birds and Fishes. June 20, 2004.
Dividing Waters. August 17, 2003. Also included in Literary Trails of the North Carolina Piedmont (UNC Press, 2010).

North Carolina Literary Review.
Clear Channel. 2017.

Panoply, A Literary Zine.
Pairing Mantids. January 2, 2021.
—Reprinted in O.Henry Magazine and Pinestraw Magazine. March, 2021.

The Phare.
Can Crows Kiss? November/December 2020.

Pine Songs.
Start the Game. 2018.

Poetry.
Better Tomorrow. June, 1993.

Prime Number Magazine. Issue 197.
Ireland as Seen From a Porch Swing in Hickory, NC. July 1, 2021

Red Fez.
At Seventy. January 2020.
How Firm a Foundation. May, 2021.
The Impossibility of America. January 14, 2021.
On An Okra Flower. 2018.
—Reprinted in O.Henry Magazine, Pinestraw Magazine, and
Walter Magazine. July, 2021.
Poem in Which I Forget Myself. January 14, 2021.
Red Clay Way. May, 2021.
To a Certain Feeling of Optimism. August, 2020.
To Very Small Devices. August, 2020.

Redheaded Stepchild.
Firing Pottery on the Night Before Winter Solstice. Fall 2020.

Silver Birch Press. Still Waiting Series.
Still Waters. April 20, 2021.

Snapdragon.
Against Desirelessness. November 2019.
Scavengers. December 2019.

The South Shore Review.
When The Shadow Took the Day Off. March 7, 2021.

South Writ Large.
Bee Fall. Spring 2020.
Beach at Corolla, NC. Spring 2020.

Speckled Trout Review.
Skinnydip in the Mill Pond. December 2019.
Swifts. May, 2021.

Third Wednesday Magazine.
The Happiness of Fear. Summer 2020.
An Honest Talk To The Shadow. Summer 2020.

Thoughts on the Power of Goodness.
Rising with the Moon on Advent Eve. December, 2020.

Turtle Island Quarterly.
Early Fall Full Moon. January 2020.

Unbroken Journal.
The Church of Misdirected Saints. July 2020.
Pig's Eye. July 2020.

Vox Poetica Magazine.
Slugs. Spring 2020.

Wine Cellar Press.
Hot Now! An Ode to Krispy Kreme Doughnuts. July, 2021

Thanks

To my best first readers, critics, and much needed copy editors in the Black Socks Poetry Group: JS Absher, Grey Brown, Ralph Earl, Janis Harrington, Maura High, Debra Kaufman, and Florence Nash.

To the poetic inspirations behind several of these poems: WB Yeats, Yuan Mei (as translated by JP Seaton in "I Don't Bow to Buddhas"), Dafydd ap Gwilym, Thomas Treherne, Robert Herrick, Petrarch (in versions from Thomas Wyatt and others), Christopher Smart, Wm Shakespeare (father of us all), Fredrico Garcia Lorca, George Herbert, Philip Larkin, Tom Lux, and the biological poetics of Roger Tory Peterson. Just to name a very few.

To the editors whose journals are mentioned in the Acknowledgments.

To the good folks at Redhawk Publications for taking on this project, Robert Canipe and Patty Thompson.

To those in my life in various ways who forgive a man who thinks with his heart as his heart is not always wise.

About the Author

Paul Jones has published poetry in many journals as well as in cookbooks, in travel anthologies, in collections about passion, love, and in *The Best American Erotic Poems: 1800 - Present* (from Scribner). Recently, he was nominated for two Pushcart Prizes and two Best of the Web Awards. His chapbook is *What the Welsh and Chinese Have in Common*.

A manuscript of his poems crashed on the moon's surface in 2019.

Jones is Vice President of the Board of Trustees of the North Carolina Writers Network, a Board Member of the North Carolina Poetry Society, and a member of the Carrboro Poets Council.

Jones is Professor Emeritus at the University of North Carolina - Chapel Hill's School of Information Science. He holds an MFA from Warren-Wilson College.

In November 2021, he was inducted into the North Carolina State University's Computer Science Hall of Fame.

www.ingramcontent.com/pod-product-compliance
Lightning Source LLC
Chambersburg PA
CBHW030509100426
42813CB00002B/402